Ancient Greece

Teaching Tips

White Level 10
This book focuses on developing reading independence, fluency, and comprehension.

Before Reading
- Ask readers what they think the book will be about based on the title. Have them support their answer.

Read the Book
- Encourage readers to read silently on their own.
- As readers encounter unfamiliar words, ask them to look for context clues to see if they can figure out what the words mean. Encourage them to locate boldfaced words in the glossary and ask questions to clarify the meaning of new vocabulary.
- Allow readers time to absorb the text and think about each chapter.
- Ask readers to write down any questions they have about the book's content.

After Reading
- Ask readers to summarize the book.
- Encourage them to point out anything they did not understand and ask questions.
- Ask readers to review the questions on page 23. Have them go back through the book to find answers. Have them write their answers on a separate sheet of paper.

© 2024 Booklife Publishing
This edition is published by arrangement with Booklife Publishing.

North American adaptations © 2024 Jump!
5357 Penn Avenue South
Minneapolis, MN 55419
www.jumplibrary.com

Library of Congress Cataloging-in-Publication Data is available at www.loc.gov or upon request from the publisher.

ISBN: 979-8-88996-924-2 (hardcover)
ISBN: 979-8-88996-925-9 (paperback)
ISBN: 979-8-88996-926-6 (ebook)

Decodables by Jump! are published by Jump! Library.
All rights reserved. No part of this book may be reproduced in any form without written permission from the publisher.

Photo Credits
Images are courtesy of Shutterstock.com. With thanks to Getty Images, Thinkstock Photo and iStockphoto. Cover – tilialucida. 4–5 – ivan bastien, Daniel Eskridge. 6–7 – Dimitrios P, Davide Catoni. 8–9 – Gilmanshin, vkilikov. 10–11 – nightcap, fizkes. 12–13 – Mark Christopher Cooper, HalynaRom. 14–15 – Maryna Kulchytska, Kozlik. 16–17 – Unknown man, Eroshka. 18–19 – Fedor Selivanov, Massimo Todaro. 20–21 – ArtFamily, Anastasios71.

Table of Contents

Page 4   Ancient Greece

Page 6   The Gods

Page 8   Family

Page 10   Homes

Page 12   Food

Page 14   Clothes

Page 16   Health and Medicine

Page 18   School and Learning

Page 20   Being a Kid

Page 22   Index

Page 23   Questions

Page 24   Glossary

Ancient Greece

The ancient Greeks lived more than 3,000 years ago. Ancient Greece did not just include the country we call Greece today. It also included other parts of Europe, Egypt, and Asia. Today, we still use many things that came from ancient Greece.

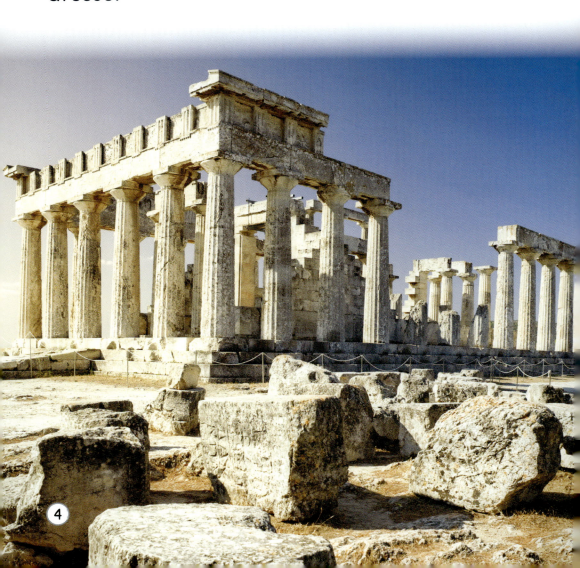

It is thanks to the ancient Greeks that we have things such as theater and even the Olympic Games. The Greek Olympics were sporting events that took place in a city called Olympia to celebrate a god called Zeus.

Zeus, god of thunder

The Gods

The ancient Greeks had many gods. They believed gods and goddesses helped create the world and had a say in what happened in it. If something bad happened to you, the ancient Greeks thought the gods were punishing you for doing something bad.

To make the gods like them, ancient Greeks prayed to statues of the gods. Sometimes, they even used animals as **sacrifices**. There were many stories about the gods and goddesses. Today, these stories are known as Greek **mythology**.

Medusa is a character from Greek mythology.

Family

In ancient Greek families, the women were in charge of looking after the home. They had to cook, clean, and take care of the children. There was a lot of work to be done around the house, so children were expected to do lots of **chores** to help.

The men in ancient Greek families did not do much work around the house. Instead, they would go out and work. Even when the men were not working, they were often not at home. They would spend their time going out with their friends.

Homes

Ancient Greek homes were often made from wood and mud bricks. They did not have much furniture inside, and poor homes might not have had any decoration or paint to hide the muddy walls. Not only did houses not have decorations, but they did not even have toilets!

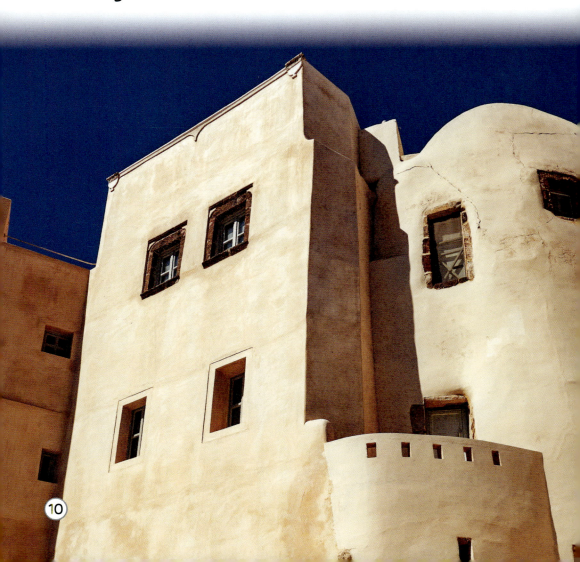

There was no electricity in ancient Greece, so the only light at night came from candles or oil lamps. Most ancient Greeks went to bed as soon as it got dark. Most families shared a bed, so all the brothers, sisters, parents, and grandparents would be in bed together.

Food

In ancient Greece, people ate lots of fruit, vegetables, and grains, such as bread. These foods were easy to grow and cheap to buy. Most ancient Greeks did not eat much meat. Meat cost a lot of money, so only very rich people could buy and eat it.

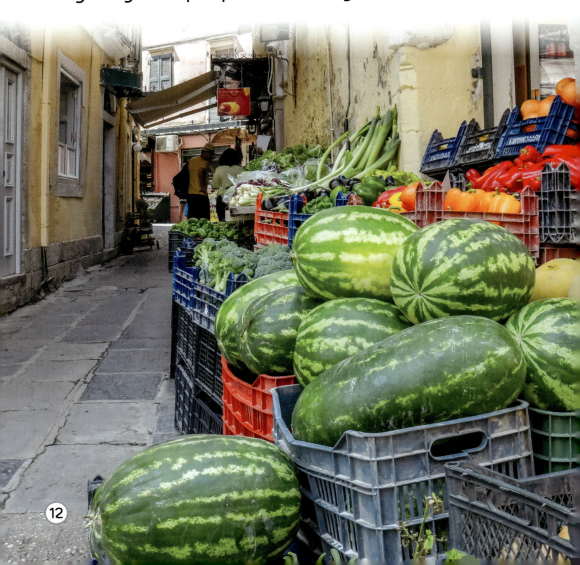

The way people ate their food was different in ancient Greece. They did not have knives and forks. Instead, everyone ate with their fingers. Food was often cut up in the kitchen to make it easier to eat, but it was still a lot messier than eating today!

Clothes

It was very hot in ancient Greece, so people wore clothes that kept them cool. Most people wore tunics. A tunic was a thin piece of cloth, like a sheet. Men wore tunics that went down to their knees, while women's tunics went down to their feet.

When children were young, they did not wear full tunics. They just wore a short piece of cloth around their middle. Popular hairstyles changed throughout ancient Greece. However, many statues showed ancient Greeks with curly hair. Ancient Greeks used **beeswax** to keep their curls in place!

Health and Medicine

Today, we have **vaccines** to stop us from getting ill and medicine to take if we do get sick. They did not have these things in ancient Greece. There are many **illnesses** that would not be a problem for us today but would have been very dangerous to the ancient Greeks.

The ancient Greeks did interesting things when people got sick. For example, doctors believed that having too much or not enough liquid in your body could make you sick. They might take out some of your blood to try and heal something completely different, such as a pain in your side!

School and Learning

In ancient Greece, only boys were allowed to go to school. Oftentimes, the boys were from rich families. They started school when they were seven years old. They learned how to read, write, and do math. Boys also did many physical activities. Many classes were outside.

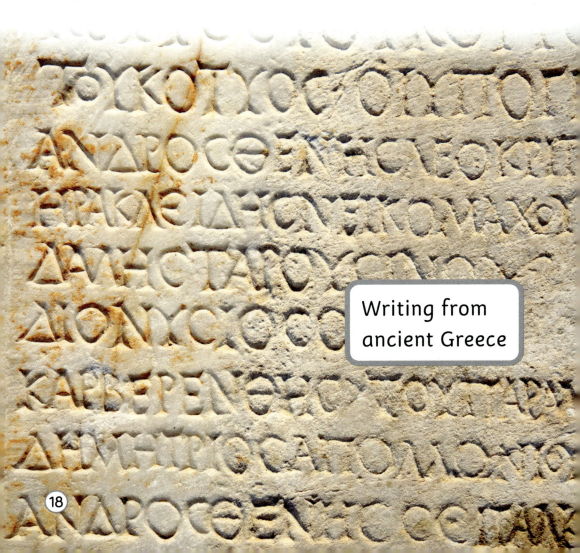

Writing from ancient Greece

Girls learned from their mothers. They were taught how to sew. They also learned how to cook and take care of the house.

Being a Kid

Depending on whether you were a boy or a girl, and even depending on where you lived, childhood in ancient Greece could be very different. At around 12 years old, girls were treated like adults! This meant getting rid of all their toys and even getting married.

In a place called Sparta, children did not belong to their parents. Instead, they were taken away and raised to become soldiers. At age seven, boys were forced to join the Spartan army. They were put through some very harsh tests that were meant to make them strong.

Index

fruit 12
math 18
Medusa 7
Olympic Games 5

soldiers 21
toilets 10
tunics 14–15

How to Use an Index

An index helps us find information in a book. Each word has a set of page numbers. These page numbers are where you can find information about that word.

Example: balloons 5, 8–10, 19

Important word

Page numbers

This means page 8, page 10, and all the pages in between. Here, it means pages 8, 9, and 10.

Questions

1. What city did the Olympic Games take place in during ancient times?

2. What foods did the ancient Greeks eat?

3. How was education different for boys and girls in ancient Greece?

4. Using the Table of Contents, can you find what page you can read about health and medicine in ancient Greece?

5. Using the Index, can you find a page in the book about soldiers?

6. Using the Glossary, can you define what mythology is?

Glossary

beeswax:
A waxy substance made by bees.

chores:
Tasks that need to be done often.

illnesses:
Sicknesses.

mythology:
A collection of stories that belongs to a certain religion or culture.

sacrifices:
Offers to a god or goddess.

vaccines:
Injections that help the body fight diseases.